BEING ONE

Shivani Dhar

BookLeaf Publishing

India | USA | UK

Made with ❤ on the BookLeaf Publishing Platform
www.bookleafpub.in
www.bookleafpub.com

Dedication

To my friends and family without whom this book would have been completed seven years ago... and to the ever annoying pigeons of Ahmedabad city who never ceased laying eggs in my balcony, keeping me at work bring up their kids. The Langurs and the langur like neighbourhood children who kept damaging my car, ringing my doorbell for no particular reason and keeping my mojo to fight back alive...

Preface

Poetry is a quiet bridge between the unsaid and the
understood. It reaches beyond words, beyond language,
into something we all carry—fragments of memory,
unspoken thoughts, fleeting moments of wonder.
The poems in this book are not just mine; they belong to
anyone who has ever paused to feel, to question, to
dream. They are for those who have carried too much,
who have searched for meaning in the ordinary, who
have found music in the silence. Some will feel like a
mirror, others like a distant echo of something you once
knew but forgot.
This collection is an offering—not as answers, but as
reminders. That we are all connected. That words are
living things. And that within them, we might find a
glimpse of ourselves.

Welcome to these pages, where emotions unfold,
untamed and unfiltered.

— Shivani

Acknowledgements

No work comes into being in isolation. These poems, though born in solitude, have been shaped by the presence of many—those who have inspired, challenged, and encouraged me along the way.
To the voices that have echoed in my mind, the books that have left their imprint, and the moments of quiet revelation—I am grateful. To the friends who listened, the loved ones who believed, and the fleeting conversations that sparked new ideas, thank you.
And to you, dear reader, for opening these pages and stepping into this world of words—this book is as much yours as it is mine.

With gratitude,
Shivani

1. Torn genes!

The crucial role of human stupidity
Is to keep alive its turbidity

Because I am a human being
Carrying all its corruptions in my genes

I don't leave a thing without a mark
Ode to my hunger to be seen stark

Among many roles I have been cast
As statue of Liberty chaos I have caused

I rose even higher to a cause called Unity
Still not visible to Mars, what a pity

Do I have enough metal in my core
To keep going further more

Or should I call it quits and hug my sanity
Maybe I just missed the point bleakly

And got carried away by divine trickery
When all it needed from me was a bit Maturity

Well now since I know this wisdom
The younger ones are born in cauldron

Long detached from the fairy humdrum
These tales of past don't help them

Their hearts broken, they carry a broken mind
The very meaning of life they don't find

Maybe fairytales weren't that bad a deal
To spell love, once was a way to heal

2. Sunscreen Blues

The smell of sunscreen on my skin
Takes me to a world where skies begin
And meet the water at the horizon's line
A stretch of warm sand, white crystalline

Tiny shells, magnificently formed
Their secrets held where the ocean swarmed
Starfish and coral, scattered in peace
While scallops rest where the waters cease

The salty breeze lifts my hair and sighs
Frizzy drinks in hand, bottles rise
With cheerful clinks, a toast to the sun
As golden rays bake loaves—day undone

We lie in the warmth, our bellies down
Kids buzzing 'round with feathered crown
Colourful butterflies kiss the earth
In the quiet, they dance in mirth

Sandcastles rise, and mermaids hide
As orange gives way to the evening tide
The sun dips low, a fading hue
And distant boats disappear from view

They pull their nets, like stories old
A daily trade in the sea's soft fold
Waves come and go, like whispered prayer
Kissing my feet with a gentle smear

3. Misty mountain walks

In the mist, where the deodars rise
The world stands still beneath the skies
Roots in the earth, reaching deep
While inside me, the storms won't sleep

The fog rolls in, soft and cold
A quiet peace, a story untold
But inside, there's noise and fire
A restless heart, a wild desire

A beam of light breaks through the grey
A touch of warmth to start the day
But my mind's a storm, a tangled mess
Chasing dreams, too hard to guess

The flowers dance with every breeze
Swaying so easy, lost in ease
And I'm a ship lost on the sea
Torn between what's wild and free

The ground is rich with autumn's gift
The trees, they shed, the winds they lift
But I carry weight that slows my pace
Looking for light, lost in space

Yet in this forest, calm and still
I find a whisper, assuring and real
Maybe peace is just a spark
A place to rest when life gets dark

For in the silence, I can see
That calm and chaos are part of me
Like fire and rain, they come and go
A part of the dance, the ebb and flow

4. Waves of Light

I've been chasing shadows in the night
But the stars don't burn as bright
I'm still looking for something I can't define
A little peace, a little sign

But everywhere I turn, it's all a blur,
I see the smiles, but can't trust what they were
A glance, a whisper, and the truth slips through
The people I know, now unrecognisable too

I dive a little deeper, then I see the cracks
The masks we wear, the things we lack
And the faces I've loved, they start to twist
In the maze of secrets, something's amiss

Who do I trust when it's all smoke and glass
When kindness is shallow, and the moment won't last
The hearts I thought were open, now locked away
As I search for honesty, but it's led astray

Like a woodchuck digging in the dirt
I burrow deeper, but it only hurts
I dig for truth, but the earth is thick
And I'm stuck in a cycle I can't fix

The world spins faster, yet I stand still
Caught in the tug of an unseen will
I'm feeling my way through this fractured maze
Wishing I could see through the fog and haze

But I'll keep searching, keep asking why
Even when the answers feel like a lie
And though the sun fades, it'll rise again
I'll find my truth, beyond the pain

Somewhere in the chaos, there's a spark
A reason to move, a place to start
We're all just waves, lost in the fight
But we keep reaching, still seeking the light

5. Tiptoeing soul of divine: Motifs of joy woven in fabric of time

A second, a second, a second
and another
A cross, a cross, a cross
yet another
I exist in these overlaps forever
Not in years, months, days or minutes altogether
Six Red, two pink, eight blue
and another
Six Red, two pink, eight blue
yet another
I exist in this symphony forever
Not in pink, red, blue or any other hue altogether
A petal, a vein, a thorn
and another
A bud, a bulb, a bloom
yet another
I exist in the essence forever

Not in an insect, a being or flora altogether
A rose, a leaf, a branch
and another
A bee, a bug, a bird
yet another
I exist in these gardens forever
Not at a spot, tip-toeing from one to the other

6. Wired to Tomorrow

We're breathing in the digital light
Thoughts drifting like satellites
No wires, no walls, no lines between
Just waves of truth, so vast, unseen

Voices hum on endless streams
Floating through the spaces between
The world we built, now set afloat
Every soul a tiny note

The future's carved in shifting skies
We search for answers, ask the why
Are we the dreamers or the dream
What does it mean to flow in the beam

Are we the echoes of tomorrow
Or the voices yet to call
A spark is never just a spark
It's the fire we'll become, after all

We're flying on the currents of time
No wires to trace our climb
Boundless air and open eyes
Touch the stars, we never fall

The code's inside, but we are free
In the silence, we still speak
Wired to tomorrow, we don't need a name
We'll rise above, beyond the frame

The world is heavy with its choice
But we're finding strength in every voice
As robots weave the threads we missed
We learn to dream, we learn to exist

Hands that once held steel and stone
Now trace the maps that we've outgrown
In every mind, a world anew
What if we're all the answer too

Are we the echoes of tomorrow
Or the voices yet to call
A spark is never just a spark
It's the fire we'll become, after all

We're flying on the currents of time
No wires to trace our climb

Boundless air and open eyes
Touch the stars, we never fall

The code's inside, but we are free
In the silence, we still speak
Wired to tomorrow, we don't need a name
We'll rise above, beyond the frame

No more strings to tie us down
We wear the sky, we wear the crown
In the silence, we begin again
gathering in hope all our pain

Tomorrow's rhythm's in our hands
Rocking future like our favourite bands
We're not just sparks, we're the fire
In every heartbeat, in every wire

Tomorrow's call is already here
We'll meet it with no fear
Wired to tomorrow
Where we go, we're already near

7. Unwritten and Unpainted

I look around, and I see the light
In faces, in books, in endless flights

Each flicker of hope, a thread I crave
Each dream a path I long to brave

But none of them feels like home
Not the artist, not the sage, not the poet alone

I'm not just one, not just one theme
Fragments of every untold dream

A painter, a singer, a wanderer, a saint
But none of these calls without restraint

And here inside me, the poet weeps
Her words like rivers, in torrents, they sweep

She whispers, "I have stories to tell"
But the artist, she yells, "You do not know me well!"

The artist demands to break the frame
To paint the world, to create the flame

"Don't you see?" she says, "I need to be free!"
But the poet's voice is louder, she won't let me be

They fight in silence, in my heart
Each one pulling me, tearing me apart

The poet in her quiet rage
The artist desperate to leave the cage

When one takes over, the other screams
Their voices tangled in mysterious dreams

If I live too long in words and rhyme
The artist's fury stops the hands of time

Her canvas cries out in bitter woe
While the poet's quill refuses to flow

But if the brush controls my soul
The poet shrieks, "This isn't whole!"

And when they battle for too long
My body goes still, like an unspoken song

I can't move, I can't breathe, I can't see
Lost between them, who will I be

For days I stay in this frozen trance
Too torn to dance, too numb to glance

A writer, a painter, an endless war
Each one claiming what's mine, wanting more

I know they'd make me an interesting tale
A character for movies, but I'm too frail

These battles inside are too much to take
I'm breaking slowly, for my own sake

Are we the echoes of tomorrow
Or the voices yet to call

A spark is never just a spark
It's the fire we'll become, after all

We're flying on the currents of time
No wires to trace our climb

Boundless air and open eyes
Touch the stars, we never fall

The code's inside, but we are free
In the silence, we still speak

Wired to tomorrow, we don't need a name
We'll rise above, beyond the frame

8. Dark roast with honey on side!

Perched upon the sill, I wait
Wings flutter light, a whispered gait
The morning light, it kisses me
As I watch her brew with quiet glee

A fragrant wave begins to rise
Like flowers blooming 'neath blue skies
The air, alive with notes so deep
A brewing scent that stirs from sleep

The warmth unfurls, like embers bright
It draws me closer with a soft might
I taste the air, its bitter-sweet
A promise held in every beat

She stirs the cup with hands so deft
A steady grace, an owner's heft
The taste, both rich and velvet-smooth
A note that sparks, that starts to move

Her eyes begin to wander far
Into the brew, where thoughts unbar
They soar and dip in shades of blue
Like endless skies, serene and true

Each sip she takes, her soul takes flight
A world unfolds in gentle light
The deep, dark brew, the subtle sweet
It whispers dreams both bright and fleet

I flutter near the window sill
As she sips deeper, time stands still
The warmth, the taste, they intertwine
A world of wonder, musical divine

Her thoughts like colors start to swirl
In hues of blue, pink and purple
The coffee's kiss, it calls her near
And takes her far, without a fear

The holding warmth, the soft release
It swells the air with magical peace
I drift, a whisper on the breeze
A silent witness to her fierce ease

9. Gourd Gala

The towering vine-like egos are clipped at the nip
Then they shoot sideways and are born females, heavy-
hipped
It's time for spring gala...
Heart-whole, this bug goes around singing love notes—
ooo la la...

Men are no priests, but they shrive, and women shiver
The petals close, and their heavy bottoms quiver
Flower becomes a fruit and grows bigger
First green, then they begin to color

Yellow, orange, brown, spotted... Some wild, some sober
Fellow beings are invited to sing and dance together
They make merry and pluck our children
Leaving the umbilical cord bleeding forever

The gala is no less than an illusion
It's a spring in odd time and without any reason

They often miss the centre of this musical ringing
For their deaf ears can only hear their own singing
Calliopean! Calliopean! Calliopean!
Let'em go...if weather stays clement, we shall be again
offspringing...

While the entire farm looked amused
Hearing the fate that they'd perused
Tara sat quiet, eyes turned away
Not quite thrilled to dance and sway

Her mind was blooming, wild and free
"What if this gala's not for me?
What lies beyond this vine-clad spree?
What's past the gates of Gourd City?"

Pale she looked... a frail child...
Barely fed, and questions she was raising
Were too heavy for her own bearing...

"Sparkling windows of magic twinkle in time...
If you manage to peep through once as they shine...
You are freed forever!
From the cycles of hard and soft, day and night, good
and bad
And you shine forever in eternity... A shining star you
become... Tara!"

"How do I peep in then?"
The fairy, with a vulpine smile, turned away...
"O child... O child... O sweet child o' mine
You have to LIGHT UP! And shed your carry-on
The mud of old, the air of new
And the teeny-weeny tendrils you cling to
Carry only the essence of you
And see how fast you move!
Innocent flowers like you have leapt miles
On the golden map of boundaries
Rendering the lines dull every time they crossed these
Only essence! Only essence! Only essence!
The gourds travel the Americans, the Europeans, and
now the Indians
Mixing leads to a delightful variety—
Pumpkins, bottle, bitter gourds, and the exotic zucchini!
For what is in micro is in the macro,
Take these and SHIVOO on the flying shoe..."

And at night... they appear...
The sparkling windows of magic, all at once, in all
forms...
She flies higher, pondering over her recent discoveries
Though happy to see her kin meet their desired destinies
"Not the Gourd Gala, but to make a new family
I want to fly to another country"

Free from the lines of good and bad
As she LIT UP! and shed her carry-ons
The fairy's voice echoed in the canyon
"ELATE! Puff up your orange pride so high
Let your Gourd Gowns kiss the sky"

It's spring once more, yet none can see
A bloom that stirs internally
And I shall freeze you, just stay there
Locked in joy beyond compare

Captured bright in time's embrace
A glow that nothing can erase
For only laughter, light, and cheer
Shall echo loud, shall linger near

Only spring, in endless spree
Is all this world should ever see

10. The Golden cage

My gold watch won't stop to watch
Me grow as I wish to go
Being in the moment
Living the event

Not rushing through
And merely ingesting lists to do
Defecate mounds of bull shit
Take cover in soldier's pit

Marching the day every new date
Leaves of calendar turn & toss in hate
A lucky coin flung in the air to open my gate
Because they pointed up when i asked
Who's the one to write my fate

Wanted to barge in furious
Question the cruelty I bore for year
Where is my lucky charm
To save me from the harm

And my guardian angel
To guide me when I'm fragile
My golden watch has a green dial
Worn around my wrist in elegant style

It clicks with my heart beat
As my pulse matches my feet
Warm with my own heat
It says in a mundane bleat

Don't you know my creators
They made me to leap peaks & craters
I am meant to move faster than ship
Keep pace with me click-click

I am your future's call
Follow me y'all
I am the charm, I am the angel
Fall in my sweet rhythm
We'll glide past dark seas like seagull

And shine bathed in the morning sun
Sea frothing beneath our feet
We shall emerge with great feat

We were never meant for slow

Only our goals we didn't know
We have a deal of a million flights together
New seas to see, new goals to uncover

So take heed and keep your vision clear
We're heading to a nice place I swear
Now, as the gold watch clicks its final call
We leap into the wild unknown, tearing down every wall

No calendar can hold the pulse of our unchained race
For we're forged to shatter time, to redefine fate's face
Every beat echoes promises of skies unconfined
Where dreams burst forth and hope is our design

Embrace the rhythm of this cosmic, daring flight
Our hearts alight with fire, our souls igniting night
The future sings in secret chords, raw and undefined
Together we write our destiny, our own truth enshrined

So, come along—let's shatter limits with our daring art
For in each tick and pulse, we carve our legacy in the
heart

11. Braided in one!

A walk with my inner child
Hand in hand into the wild

Through the lanes of memory
From days of forgotten history

Is this memory true...
Or the lenses i am seeing it through

Treading pathways
Leaping gateways

Standing dazed
Having swept by the waves

I stood as a culprit there
In my mother's stern stare

Cold and frightened
I took the beating till the end

Now she'll hug me, now she'll kiss me
Will she not burst into tears
Seeing how much my tiny heart bears

And yearns for her warmth, her hug, her kiss
While my years pass by with a 'Big Miss'

Written all over my diary of affection
Even when I didn't have a diction

To tell my story through
But I had one for sure, I knew

I knew it when my feet cold
Made friends with my heart cold

Together they formed a world
Of their own called fridgedland
With a suspecting eye for scrutiny
no one could stand...

I turned to see, myself in front of a sea
Only me, standing in her stare

In the absence of warmth, of open arms
I had grown to bear her charms

Not just her, but the ones before
Their voices echoed in my core

The mother's mother, the daughter too
Braided tight in all I do....

Was I the child, or was I she?
The giver, the taker—now one in me

So I love too much, I give too deep
Afraid of the cold that still creeps

Afraid that if I do not burn
I will freeze, and never return

So I pour, I drown, I flood, I fall
Fearing I may not feel at all

Hand in hand, the past and I
Walked as one, asking why...

12. Rivers running apart

"You never saw my love," you say,
But I saw it there, clear as day.
I felt it deep, I held it tight,
I carried it through storm and night.

I built us a world, do you recall?
A place where time meant nothing at all.
We played in the sun, we danced in the rain,
Far from the weight of sorrow and pain.

We made it, we kept it, we fought to defend,
But you let them in, and called it the end.
You shattered the walls, let the tide rush through,
Now they've taken you—what else could I do?

"You should've been there," now you claim,
To mend the cracks, to take the blame.
To blend with your kin, to twist my truth,
To sing their songs, erase my proof.

You ask too much, yet fail to see,
You never gave enough of *you* to me.
Sixty times, I pulled you back,
Held you steady when you fell off track.

Sixty times, I fought, I stayed,
But two I missed—and that's all you weigh.
You count the falls, but not the climb,
You rewrite the tale to fit your rhyme.

Your love bends toward them, not me,
Your brother, your friends—you let them see.
But I was the one who stood by your side,
Now just an empty shell, cast aside.

So take what's left, the scraps, the whole,
You've drained my heart, you've drained my soul.
And when you turn, when you are through,
There'll be no more of me for you.

From the same storm, we both arose,
Yet walked such different paths of woes.
Our truths like rivers, running apart,
A miracle we even let love start.

For all the sunsets we saw together
The ones we saw as friend I cherish forever

If nothing else, one thing is true,
You loved me once, and I loved you too...

13. Butterfly

Tiny magnificence
Fluttering around blades
Of tender grass green...
Dash of yellow sprinkled
Here and there in
Dots and strokes
Across the canvas
White and brown upon
Washes of blue
French, Navy, Cerulean

14. A Bloom beyond the branch!

A flower unfurls slow, a whisper
petals parting, dreams delivered
It stands in silence, yet it speaks
in velvet touch and fragrant streaks

It does not beg, it does not plead
it sways where sun and shadow meet
Yet if one dusk, it lets go
not plucked, not lost, but choosing so

Then know it left with quiet grace
trading branch for your embrace
Not severed, not stolen—just set to roam
seeking a life beyond its home

Now it lingers in your palm
unbound, yet exuding charm
Will you let it dim, dissolve
or let its beauty ever evolve

For in your hands, it lives much more
than ever tied to its vine before
No longer bound, no longer still
but shaping life in ways it willed

It watches softly while you dream
rests where the gold light gleams
By your table, near your bed
its presence lingers, love spreads

No matter if the world forgets
if glances pass, if hearts neglect
It'll smile at you with sunshine bloom
Through silent nights and golden noon

And so, it'll find its meaning too
not just for you—but for itself anew

15. Weaving inner gardens into carpets

Here in this carpet lives an ever lovely spring
Unscrorched by summer's ardent flame
Safe too from autumn's boisterous gale
Is gaily blooming still

The handsome wide border is the garden wall
Protecting, preserving the park within
For refuge and renewal—a magic space
For concourse, music, and joyful din

Where blossoms dance in the morning light
And lanterns glow through velvet night
A haven bright, both wild and free
A world of bloom, a woven melody

We're halfway through to our garden of dreams
Where effort blooms in golden gleams
A park of contrast, bold and bright
Where harmony sings in shade and light

More than before, yet less than beyond
A fleeting rest where time is drawn
A breath, a pause, a hush so slight
Before we march to morning's sight

At last, we reach the sacred ground
Where love's own whispers now resound
Will it rise—a Tree of Life
Or baroque wonders rich and rife
Or shall it stand, in soft repose
A vase of blooms, a love that grows

For contemplation's lonely spell
Conversations grave or lover's shy disclosure
From all these perils at last set free
In this garden all find security

The beloved's face at last we see
And there attain our journey's end
Our life's reward and final destiny
Refuge and fulfilment in his infinity

16. Let's step out and see

We long to belong, to be held, to be known
Wrapped in the weave of a life we've outgrown
A home, a name, a space to exist
But too many ties, and we start to resist

We break away—mountains call, deserts sigh
We chase open skies, let the wind pull us high
Yet freedom feels hollow when echoes return
Isolation's a fire that chills as it burns

We're drops in an ocean, alone yet entwined
Seeking the comfort of ties we maligned
We need a cradle, a tether, a thread
A reason to stay, a place to be fed

The first box we build is the one in our chest
A ribcage of shelter where hearts come to rest
But it's never enough—so we fashion it wings
Give it motion, give it speed, let it cling to new things

Feet on the ground, but our minds slip away
Wandering further, refusing to stay
We escape one cage just to craft one anew
A planet, a border, a limitless view

Now Earth is too small, too known, too near
We've made it our home, but it's time to veer
We turn to the stars, to Mars, to the Moon
Shopping through space like explorers in bloom

A cosmic thrift store, no price, just a fare
Pay for the ride, and once you are there
It's all yours to claim, to carve, to confine
To build up new walls and redraw the lines

Because even in flight, even set free
We tether ourselves to what we can see
We stretch and expand, but always remain
Caged in our need to belong once again

Some shape their boxes with effortless flair
So seamless, we welcome them, place them with care
Others feel heavy, just taking up space
Waiting to shift, to be replaced

But the beautiful ones, like this *Kalamdani*
Hold stories untold, wild and uncanny

A vessel of dreams, a door to explore
A key to worlds unseen before

Yet a *Kalam* in the wrong embrace
Might twist the truth, might lose its grace
Only hands that see what's true
Can let it speak the way it's meant to

17. Pink

From my window, I'd watch them bloom,
Those soft pink swirls, filling up the room.

Big as my face, glowing so bright,
They felt like stories of magic and delight.

I'd press my face into their velvet soft,
Taking in their beauty, never enough.

The air sweet like honey, warm and gold,
A tranquil moment in time to behold.

Their petals, a tender labyrinth unfold,
A portal to a world, a story so bold,

I'd imagine myself a dewdrop there,
Resting on them, floating in the air.

No struggle, no effort for all that grace,
A bush turning into a wild, bright space.

Hundreds of roses, full and free,
Filling my heart with a kind of glee.

Each bloom whispered, "It'll all be okay,"
A quiet promise that hope would stay.

But as I left, far from home,
I took their scent, their softness, to roam.

Their light still lingers deep in my chest,
A quiet whisper, a love manifest.

Now, I carry these memories close,
A pink glow, a gift from the pink rose.

18. Pita and Feta

It's flatulently flavoursome
How feta got fatter
And fatter wore feather
To flatter
Wore to tatter
And tatter his chords to shatter
Feta got fatter
And fatter got no better
Only rattle
Dipped in batter
With kin cheddar
Made pita the pro hatter
Filled with the matter
Some tossed on platter
And on walls some splatter
No flatter
Only rattle
A box of chatter
That only got better

Served on platter
This creamy matter

19. We are One

Thinking exists
within the confines of a mind.
Mindfulness overflows
to the eternal realms of love
and awareness,
of oneness.
Thinking no more remains
a mechanical job work
of an inadequate apparatus
in isolation.
It becomes more
of living togetherness
and has often found peasants
huddled up beneath the shafts
of linguistic flags,
awaiting their alms
of borrowed words,
ignorant about their own existence,
so connected and so fashioned
by everything and everyone.

20. What's the floss!

Swooshed across my balcony, was I held afloat?
I don't need jet planes, don't need a boat

Caught in the world-wind, had I lost my path?
Sugar grain dissolving in a hot stirring bath

Beyond, there is a glorious fair
A vision fell like a saving snare

All apparel shed as I cruised through memory lane
A light between lights... of a kindled flame

Bright crackling fireworks dazzeling on dark sky
A whirlwind of crystalline flakes ahead of my eyes

Swirling around an axis, a fine fluff of astral heat
Forgive my candour, was nothing but a cotton candy
treat

I say, why should you interest anything I say

When the candy man himself is churning the milky way

Garnered for the floss are tots, all shape and size
Staring at galaxies with broad melting eyes

All this he spun singing the dark night pass
A silver-tongued guy savoring fresh candy floss

21. Did I carry it all...

Has anything that I've carried
ever been of use really?
Or is the use stimulated
by the sensation of carrying?

A synesthesia caught within,
the bag of my tanned skin

A tinted glass for a shaded view shouting loud - Me too!
Oh yes you!
For days amiss my clear vision has missed you

A greasy stick for berrylike lip
is instrumental in keeping optimistic
Traced down each time by your fruity linger,
this perfidious lover has worn you thick

Mint taffies for a breezy breath,
you rattle in your case - Right & Left!
A noisy sidekick in a quiet cubical

My passion has no need for this lousy seth

Some tools of scraping, plucking & cutting,
brushes and pens for art making
Toning & shading the skin of a paper,
a stationer's pile for a Gardner's pruning

Come by essential, end up only a lavish frill,
some entangled chords, a bunch of faded bills
An antique neck piece,
sleeping in the grave of a pocket in peace

Some padded paper for notes
A tiny book of quotes
A wallet not so fat
A rubber stamp & an ink-pad

Tiny packets of vapour rubs,
for wet kisses and warn hugs
A pretty roll-on perfume cruet
A hand mirror for a frisky go-ahead

Chew-able tablets of orange flavour,
reached out seldom with little fervour
A tube to provide and two to prevent,
moisture, suntan and frizzy split ends

Saved up sachets of spicy sprinkles,
licking'em gives me goose pimples
Leaf of Red round sticker for a holy look
A tiny pack of dry & salted drupe

A lovely little sun hat
Bunch of keys & a lot of this that
Everyday holus bolus I leave home in meh
As it happens to be a sunny swimming day...